Perspectives of Supply Chain Competitiveness— A Handbook

An Evaluation of Supply Chain Growth, Literature, Framework for Assessment and Vulnerabilities in Gaining a Competitive Advantage

Dr. Zal Phiroz

ABOUT THE AUTHOR

Dr. Zal Phiroz is an expert on global supply chain management and a professor specializing in supply chain analytics, operations management and data analytics. Faculty appointments within the area of supply chain management have included University of California San Diego, Harvard University, and University of Southern California.

In addition to several years of industry experience at Procter & Gamble, Dr. Phiroz consults on supply chain projects with various Fortune 500 firms, and engages in litigation consulting on product liability and injury, vulnerabilities in manufacturing, distribution, and quality assurance. He has spoken at numerous international conferences including OPAL, Intermodal, and ByPi, and is regularly invited as a guest lecturer on industry related supply chain topics.

In addition to several supply chain and procurement designations, Dr. Phiroz holds a PhD in Supply Chain Management (Hierarchical decision making patterns for the placement of physical supply chain entities), MBA, BS Honors (Computer Information Systems), BCS (Computer Science).

CONTENTS

Competitiveness Within a Supply Chain

How does a company remain competitive in the global market? The simplicity of this question defies a single answer. A common strategy is to find ways to improve the speed and functionality of the supply chain. Speed, innovation, consumer research, attention to social causes, and meeting product requirements are some of the other objectives for which supply chains have evolved to meet. In an ever-changing arena in which consumer markets are constantly evolving, the effectiveness and efficiency of a supply chain must consider a variety of success metrics.

Some of the traditional core areas of potential optimization may include:

- Warehousing

- Transportation

- Inventory management

- Materials handling

- Operations

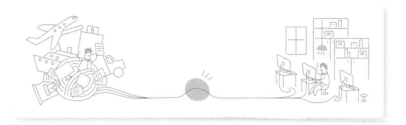

An efficient supply chain process is expected to increase its range of responsibilities in the fulfillment process. Some of these functions are:

- Monitoring customer service

- Processing and ordering in the customer service department

- Forecasting of the supply chain management budget

These areas of focus may also lead to an assessment of sub-core areas including computing and IT system processes, production and distribution simulation, operational improvements, demand projection optimization, and distribution strategy, among others under the umbrella of supply chain management.

Growth and Role of Supply Chain Management

An efficient and effective supply chain plays a crucial role in the process of ensuring a product is produced, distributed, readily available, and accessible. This role is clearly reflected through the attention afforded to the overall study of supply chain management and plays a vital role in the competitiveness of firms irrespective of industry, size, and stage of development.

In a global marketplace, ever-increasing competition is changing the way companies strategize to gain competitive advantages. It's been suggested that competition in the global market is no longer between companies, but often among supply chains.[1] This perspective is noteworthy, as it illustrates the evolution of supply chain research. Earlier research largely points to a focus on how supply chain efficiency may improve specific businesses, whereas later studies focus on the overall improvement of industry supply chains. In evaluating prior literature, it becomes important for companies to understand their competitors' strategies in order to benchmark the best option to gain competitive advantage.

Supply chain management, as an umbrella term, has served to describe the various stages of critical planning and execution which are crucial to the success of any company. The concept, however, has shifted from being a generalization to being more specific, largely driven by the need to recognize the cause and source of competitive advantage. The identification of specific areas within supply chain management are often foundation points for areas of analysis and competitive advantage (e.g., inventory control or storage replenishment). Changing trends within commerce, including innovative process changing and consumer facing trends (e.g., driverless transportation, 3-D printing), all depend largely on a sustainable and well-established supply chain in order to efficiently and cost-effectively bring products into the hands of customers.

Despite the value placed on the efficiency of a supply chain, there does not exist a defined, clear definition of the term. The term is not a clear science and does not allow for a one-size-fits-all application. This is in spite of the fact that the practice of supply chain management and the board of knowledge within the area of supply chain management has always existed within the practice of commerce.

One of the more general descriptions of the concept of supply chain management can be stated as "the delivery of enhanced customer and economic value through synchronized management of the flow of physical goods and associated information from sourcing to consumption."[2] In this statement, there is the acknowledgement of the fact that an efficient supply chain management requires collaboration of both the internal workings of a company as well as the external partners of an organization. These external partners are often referred to as the extended supply chain.[3]

Other definitions of supply chain management have been defined by the streamlining of a business' supply-side activities to maximize customer value and gain a competitive advantage in the marketplace.[4] While the term "supply chain management" may focus on a company's strategic vision, the role of a supply chain differs greatly within each application in the global marketplace. Several references to supply chain management have become mainstream;[5] however, there are very few bodies of literature that concentrate solely on the concept of supply chain management. Rather, the role that supply chain management plays as a piece of a larger puzzle is greatly explored across the global marketplace. The development of the concept began along the lines of physical distribution and transport and was as a result of several overlapping concepts.

To comprehend the scope of the term, the following table is given:

Table 1: Interpretations of Supply Chain Management

Researchers	Year	Definition
Chopra and Meindl	2007	"A supply chain consists of all stages involved, directly or indirectly, in fulfilling a customer request."[6]
Mentzer *et al.*	2001	"The systemic, strategic coordination of the traditional business functions and the tactics across these business functions within the supply chain, for the purposes of improving the long-term performance of the individual companies and the supply chain as a whole."[7]
Handfield and Nichols	1999	"A supply chain encompasses all the activities with the flow and transformation of goods from the raw stage, through to the end user, as well as the associated information flows."[8]
Christopher	1998	"The supply chain is the network of organizations that are involved through upstream and downstream linkages, in the different processes and activities that produce value in the form of products and services in the hands of ultimate customer."[9]
Cox	1995	"A supply chain is a network of facilities and distribution options that performs the functions for procurement of materials, transformation of these materials intermediate and finished products, and the distribution of these finished products."[10]
Cavinato	1992	"The supply chain concept consists of actively managed channels of procurement and distribution. It is the group of firms that add value along product flow from the original raw materials and final customer."[11]
Cooper and Ellram	1993	"Supply chain management is an integrated philosophy to manage the total flow of distribution channel from the supplier to ultimate user."[12]

Gunasekaran and Ngai	2005	"Supply chain is used to refer to chain linking each element of process from raw materials through to the end customers."[13]
Towill, Naim and Wikner	1992	"The supply chains are a system, the constituent parts of which include material suppliers, production facilities, distributions services, customers linked together via the feed forward flow of materials and the feedback flow information."[14]
Lee	1996	"The integration activities taking place among a network of facilities that procure raw materials, transform them into intermediate goods and then final products, and deliver products to customers through distribution system."[15]
Morehouse and Bowersox	1995	"An integrative approach to dealing with the planning and control of the materials flow from the suppliers to end-users.[16]
Sako	1993	"The set of entities, including suppliers, logistics services providers, manufacturers, distributors, and resellers, through which materials, products and information flow."[17]
Lee and Billington	1992	"Networks of manufacturing and distribution sites that procure raw materials, transform them into intermediate and finished products, and distribute the finished products to customers."[18]
Berry et al.	1994	"Supply chain management aims at building trust, exchanging information on market needs, developing new products and reducing the supplier base to a particular OEM (original equipment manufacturer) so as to release management resources for developing meaningful, long-term relationships."[19]

By evaluating the changes in the definition over time, there appears to be a trend toward integrating the term "supply chain management" with overall corporate strategy. There does not appear to be a trend toward a more narrowly defined description, and while each definition provides an insightful aspect, the vast number of definitions inherently result in the meaning of the term being unclear.

In addition to the definition of the term, the understanding of the concept of supply chain management is still evolving and is often seen by the multitude of definitions as holding multidisciplinary origins, resulting in the lack of a clearly-defined conceptual framework. The term has not only been used to mean the integration of a company's internal and external logistics activities and the planning and controlling of materials from distributors to customers, but some authors have used the term "supply chain management" to describe strategic, inter-organization issues.[20] In some views, supply chain management is used as a term to refer to an alternative organization form to vertical integration,[21] while others referred to supply chain management simply as the relationship between the company and the suppliers.[22]

The Literature of Supply Chain Competitiveness

Irrespective of the vast number of articles written on the concept of supply chain management, the idea and the theory of the concept is not unified. Sub-concepts are often introduced as areas which categorize supply chain behavior, and which demonstrate necessary crossovers between supply chain management and other industrial and production areas.[23] Literature suggests that within an industrial district for which there is a specific production model, a complex supply chain can be clearly identified.[24]

Although the function of a supply chain has arguably always impacted the flow of commerce, arguments suggest that the success of organizations is greatly dependent on the interactions between flows of information, materials, manpower, and capital equipment.[25] Within this perspective, the concept of information flow points toward the need for automation across a supply chain. This observation is supported by noting that businesses no longer compete in isolation or independently, but as supply chains.[26] In expanding on the perception of a supply chain, it is important to note that the word "chain" should not be misunderstood to refer to a chain of businesses with a one-to-one business relationship, but rather a network or web of multiple businesses relationships. As such, a firm's "supply chain" can be identified as a way of managing business relationships within a total commerce process.

It is important to identify the benefits of an efficient supply chain. Various theories have been posed to support a company's streamlined structure, in an effort to extend competitive advantage. Inter-organizational relationships form the foundation for automation, on the assumption that the flow of commerce mirrors a network as opposed to an isolated hub. The resource-based view and knowledge-based view are two examples of managerial frameworks which can be used to explain various aspects and functional relationships. Both theoretical frameworks are well known and provide valuable insight into competitive analysis through varying perspectives of supply chain value.

Many researchers have come to conclusions regarding the need for an inter-disciplinary approach in evaluating supply chain competitiveness, in which technical and relational aspects from the respective fields of the system dynamics are integrated.[27] Product and service quality combined have a relative effect on the behavior of customers and end users who act as repeat buyers[28] and therefore have a direct effect on the supply chain's overall performance.

One particular study in 2006[29] reviewed 100 articles randomly selected out of 614 articles across nineteen years. The research addressed a variety of areas and focused on the operation management approach to supply chain management as a blanket study across a variety of industries. The result suggested a diverse application of supply chain theory, contoured to extracting competitive advantages as opposed to a unified interpretation of the practice of supply chain management.

Other research has suggested that more literature reviews were needed for the development of theoretical frameworks of supply chain management,[30] and acknowledged that more sophisticated research-modeling techniques should be used (e.g., discriminant analysis and inferential statistical techniques) in determining multiple categories in the field of supply chain management.

In evaluating theoretical frameworks, there is research which suggests building and sustaining a competitive advantage for a firm required a deeper understanding of resource utilization within a firm, which at the root can be explained as a function of supply chain automation within an organization.[31] Other research has aimed to identify broad dimensions of supply chain management and the effect on competitive advantage.[32]

Table 2: Areas of Supply Chain Management and Effect on Competitive Advantage

Categories of Supply Chain Practices	Categories and Areas of Competitive Advantage
Strategic supplier partnership	Price/Cost
Customer relationship	Quality and market share
Information sharing	Delivery dependability
Supplier network responsiveness	Time to market
Operations/Logistics responsiveness	Product innovation

From an overarching competitive advantage standpoint, it can be stated that the success of corporations and organizations is greatly dependent on the interactions between flows of information, materials, manpower, and capital equipment.[33] Further, it can be suggested that the establishment of manufacturing start-ups is mostly driven by increases in local market size and labor force qualification, lower labor costs, and a more diversified economic environment.[34] Another area of research appears to dovetail with this theory, suggesting that many global manufacturing firms may move plant locations to lower cost areas, which may also have tax benefits.[35]

A number of prior studies have investigated the impact of physical location decisions on the supply chain, with the majority of research focusing on various management, geographic, or environmental factors. While prior contributions have suggested that the function of management is central to the concept of supply chain management, relatively little attention has been placed on evaluating the correlation between location decisions and management decision drivers.[36] The analysis of this interaction would provide a comprehensive interpretation of specific factors contributing to physical supply chain development decisions.

On the previously substantiated assumption that supply chain management as a concept often forms the basis for competitive advantages between organizations, several theoretical frameworks exist in which elements of supply chain management may be discussed. The relational-based view, innovation-based view, Transactional Cost Economics theory, resource-based view, and knowledge-based view are among these frameworks.

Nature of Competition Within a Supply Chain

The concept of supply chain management is often considered to be a vital part of any production process and is part of an increasing trend which has not yet reached its full growth potential. Many of the theories and hypotheses behind the evaluation of supply chain competitiveness have explored how various aspects may come together to form a link and ultimately produce a competitive advantage. The platform for this area of analysis is described through the assessment of theoretical frameworks, whereby theories related to the study problem were discussed. The analysis of theories makes it possible to gain valuable insight and support in explaining various impacts on a supply chain.

Key gaps still exist in the overall study and analysis of the practice, as there are many areas which have not yet been explored or sufficiently researched. As industry and society progress, emerging challenges may require a focus on specific areas (e.g., driverless transportation or the impact of tracing technology on various phases of the supply chain). Various controversies and societal inadequacies may also present opportunity for specific risk assessment of supply chain research (e.g., ship transit piracy, pandemic breakouts). Further research into specific areas of optimizing, analyzing, and evaluating a supply chain presents itself as an important and necessary practice.

External and Physical Considerations for Competitive Advantage

One of the primary goals of a supply chain is to provide customers with accurate and quick responses to their orders at the lowest possible cost.[37] In order to achieve this, it is necessary for a concert of facilities to be strategically connected and consistently evolving to meet the ever-changing needs of the market. For global supply chains, coordination and customization are even more complex and require the consideration of multiple factors on multiple tiers of product development, manufacturing, distribution, retail, storage and labor—each presenting an opportunity for firms to gain competitive advantage. Other vital areas of consideration (including demand projection, transport costs between all demand and supply points within the network, fixed operating costs of each distribution or retail facility, revenue generated per customer location, facility labor, operating costs, and even construction costs[38]) may also be considered as areas of competition between firms within the realm of the supply chain.

Table 3 assesses several critical factors which require consideration when making location decisions.

Table 3: Critical Factors in Location Decisions[39]

Factors Related to Location	Factors Related to Transport	Factors Related to Utilities	Environmental and Social Factors	Political, Legal, Governance Factors
Access by customers	Convenience achieved	Availability of fuel	Adequate housing and roads	Payroll taxes
Demand and markets	Closeness to key markets	Waste disposal	Education facilities	Local and state tax structure
Sourcing	Access to sources of suppliers	Adequate supply of water	Climate and living conditions	Taxation climate and policies
Ability to access and retain labor force	Availability of diverse transport modes	Adequate supply of power	Community attitudes	Opportunity for advertisement in strategic points
Labor rates	Cost of transportation	Local energy costs	Health care facilities	Zoning laws
Location of competitors	Strategic visibility of the facility from major roads	Communications capability	Property costs	Health and safety laws
Traffic congestion around the location	Availability of parking space	Price/cost	Cost of living	Regulation agencies and policies
Access to adequate labor skills	Inbound and outbound capabilities	Utility regulatory laws and practices		Taxation incentives and abatements

As seen in the above table, physical location decisions, both for small and large brick-and-mortar businesses within the main supply chain sectors (manufacturing, distribution, and retail) are relatively complex and often correlated. Factors such as transport cost, infrastructure, or tax structure, etc., have a considerable impact on location decision. It is therefore necessary to consider how each element is affected as a result of a location decision, and therein how each decision impacts the overall supply chain. The physical location of key supply chain processes must enable and allow a business to process inventory, maintain on-time delivery, and maintain sustainability within the chain.

A number of factors may be considered as potential impacts to location decisions (e.g., geographic risk, political risk, economic risk). In order to define a specific framework, emphasis is placed on specific location factors: cost of land on which a facility is located, geometric factors of the land and surrounding geography, distance from the site to and from other various supporting facilities, cost of transportation, area demographics, and tax structure.

Prior research has focused on a variety of perspectives within the area of supply chain management. Research prior to 1975 focused on the assessment of individual corporations,[40, 41, 42] whereas much research taking place between 1975 and 1995 focused more so on the overall supply chain function.[43] In evaluating the functionality of a supply chain, physical facility placement emerges as a key source of competitive advantage, and as such, the decision process maintained in the placement of physical supply chain entities is central. Opportunity exists to further existing research in this area and to expand on opportunities for competitive advantages through supply chain refinement.

Through various studies and observation, it has been established that supply chain management constitutes a major component of competitive strategies which enhance organizational productivity and profitability,[44] while today's business environment trends often focus on exerting pressure on organizations to improve areas in which value can be added to enable a sustainable competitive advantage in the industry. From an external and physical perspective, critical areas which can be identified as competitive advantage sources include maintenance of products and services, waste assessment, inventory control, distribution structure, delivery model and customer service. One consequential result of evaluating supply chain management from a competitive perspective is identifying the need for efficient control and coordination of a supply chain, in order to ensure that the diverse needs of an organization's stakeholders are met.

Changes in the business environment and corporate trends suggest that a supply chain is a core pillar for the success of any business today, irrespective of industry or nature.[45] Further, from a physical and external perspective, supply chain management is described as a critical pillar[46] due mainly to the premise that an effective supply chain directly contributes to the productivity and growth of an organization on a macro level. It can therefore be suggested that an efficient supply chain exhibits features such as corporate profitability, employment cost reduction, production cost reduction, job security, and positive contribution to industrial growth.[47, 48, 49]

The functionality of a supply chain is heavily dependent on several key success factors including procurement strategy, effective and efficient control systems, and the development of personnel expertise. One of the main goals in the development of an effective supply chain management structure should be to respond adequately to the multiple needs of end consumers and stakeholders. In an attempt to develop a coherent and functional supply chain strategy, a business must create a supply chain which is a reflection of a sophisticated mixture of various considerations specific to the industry, scenario, business stage, and stakeholder interests of a business.[50]

There are numerous factors that contribute to the efficiency of a supply chain structure.[51] One factor is the geographical location in which land is positioned in relation to the overall supply chain strategy.[52] Supply chain design is a critical factor in supply chain competitiveness and plays a crucial role in determining the ultimate level of success of a supply chain. The determination and ultimate choice of geographical locations for supply chain operations is an important decision area for supply chain design and planning,[53] and ultimately contributes to the overall success of the corporate strategy. Factors such as labor cost, environmental impact, community acceptance, company reputation, material cost, taxation, currency exposure, and legal regulations, etc., directly affect the functionality and ultimate success of a business and are collateral results of supply chain design.

In a determination of position and flexibility, the impact of facility location within a supply chain is considered to be one of the most complex issues impacting overall efficiency.[54] Facility location decisions are heavily dependent on the industry, geographical position, and climate, and are regarded as fixed and difficult to modify.[55] Inefficient locations for production, mixing, distribution, or storage result in excess costs being incurred throughout the lifetime of the facilities (and therefore the operation of the business), irrespective of the efficiencies that may be realized with regard to production plans, transportation options, inventory management, and information-sharing decisions.[56] The variable of short-term fixed costs also must be evaluated. Decisions on production quantities, capacities, and locations, for example, are relatively more flexible, but still carry costs associated with production, and may be fixed in the short term.[57] Several factors may also depend on these decisions (e.g., labor costs).

Not all changes to a supply chain are fixed and inflexible. Areas such as transportation, inventory, and information systems have more potential to be influenced or manipulated. As a result, decisions on these areas and components may allow for a faster response to a supply chain change and an optimization of an existing chain.

Internal and Network Considerations for Competitive Advantage

Some have suggested that supply chain management as a practice has become a fundamental strategy in allowing corporations to strategically succeed, as opposed to being a core study area in itself.[58] Prior research has suggested principles which, when used consistently and comprehensively, result in competitive advantages to a company as follows:[59]

1. **Segmentation of Customers Based on Service Needs**

   Traditionally, customer segmentation was by way of industry, product, or the trade channel. Effectively optimizing a supply chain would entail grouping customers with distinct similarities and customizing demand through tailoring services for specific customer segments.

2. **Customization of the Supply Chain Network**

   As noted previously, the design of a supply chain network is crucial in ensuring that a chain operates efficiently. When designing a supply chain network, the focus should be on service needs, profitability of customers within the chain, and customization of the supply chain network accordingly. This specific principle ties all the remaining principles together by outlining guidelines on placement of supply chain entities to facilitate the effectiveness of supply chain management.

21

3. **Observation of Signals of Market Demand**

A potential corporate error is allowing fragmentation of decision-making control. Ensuring that a flat structure is utilized and assuring a multitude of teams are involved in the operations and planning stages of the supply chain allows for the detection of changes and trends in customer needs. This demand-intensive approach leads to more consistent forecasts and better resource allocation.

4. **Differentiation of Products Closer to the Customer**

Due to cost restrictions and fluctuations in demand, forecasting and inventory management is central to the efficient flow of a supply chain. As a result, product differentiation and customization become a topic which can often lead to vulnerabilities in demand projection. In order to reduce this risk, differentiation of the product in the manufacturing process should be made as close to the end of the chain as possible, in order to understand demand and meet actual customer demand.

5. **Strategical Management of the Source of Supply**

From an external perspective, the relationship between key players within a supply chain is key (e.g., suppliers, production sources, distributors, retailers etc.). Based on an understanding of supplier constraints, opportunities may exist to reduce the overall cost of purchasing materials. Decisions based on when to purchase required materials may also be impacted by cost/ supplier demand, etc.

6. **Development of a Supply Chain-Wide Technology Strategy**

Information technology in many ways may act as the cornerstone for an effective and efficient supply chain and often supports multiple levels of decision-making. An optimized supply chain strategy also gives a clear view of the flow of product to the market, as well as an indication of the reliability of services and information.

7. **Adoption of Channel-Spanning Performance Measures**

Simply monitoring internal factors and functions of a supply chain is often ineffective in optimizing an entire supply chain. Successful supply chain modification and optimization often lies in ensuring that operations strategies are outlined and clearly defined within every link in the entire supply chain.

While these principles may sound simple on paper, their execution and implementation are challenging, especially in an ever-changing supply chain landscape. It's worth noting, that research also suggests that enhanced growth is often a result of organizations accepting the need to change, as opposed to maintaining their current supply chain structure.

More recent literature suggests the literature of supply chain management is still fragmented. Despite several studies that discuss issues regarding the supply chain, most of the research that exists explains or discusses only one stage of the chain, that which is specific to an area, industry, or process.[60] A number of variables, including geography, industry, application, business size, and objective, must be considered when assessing the overall competitiveness and value of a supply chain. Business culture, for example, may present a different method of measuring and/or attributing successful implementation of a supply chain. Pertinent issues such as resource heterogeneity at the organizational level and the influence on supply chain automation must therefore be assessed. While there are multiple supply chain perspectives which form the blueprint for theoretical framework selection, the assessment of industry, size, and corporate culture helped identify a suitable theoretical framework which is adopted for the study. The objective in selection is to choose a framework based on its relevance to supply chain management, and more importantly on the ability to steer the study towards the realization of set objectives.

Perspectives and Frameworks on Supply Chain Management Competitive Advantages

From a strategic management perspective, numerous theoretical frameworks exist, with the intention of evaluating and assessing firms from the perspective of competitiveness.

The Relational-Based View

The relational-based view focuses on the measurement of an individual firm's performance within a network.[61] The core of the theory suggests that an individual firm is often unable to compete with global competition using solely their own resources and capabilities. As such, with the exception of enhancing their own core competencies, enterprises must seek out cooperation with other firms to establish relational networks. The relational networks potentially provide a firm with access to resources, markets, information, and technologies; with advantages from scale and scope economies; and will allow firms to share risks and outsource value-chain stages.[62] Overall, the framework potentially allows for firms to focus on the value chain and the division of labor. Further, firms in the network enjoy the added flexibility of not having fixed commitments to activities which are not essential; the flexibility enables firms to act more quickly than rivals, allowing firms to access key resources in their environment.[63]

Within the capacity of business optimization, investments in relationships modeling are potentially based on continuity rather than value creation. Furthermore, business network decisions involve a reduction in the supply base and the focus on strategic suppliers for the long term.

The Innovation-Based View

As a model, the innovation-based view typically evaluates independent consideration, and, together with resource-based view and knowledge-based view, enables the development of multiple theories to address the complexities of business research. A firm's knowledge contributes to creating competitive advantage which at some stage may create new knowledge to further the firm's performance by solving complex business problems, through integrating web-based data mining tools with business models for knowledge management,[64] where successful organizations build and manage knowledge effectively.[65] As a result, the argument claims that innovation can be used as a competitive benchmark, while all members of a particular organization should be able to process and manipulate knowledge. This view focuses on the role of an organization to act as a site of learning and information transfer as opposed to simply a physical site or financial entity.

Criticism of this view often follows an assessment of the value of innovation and the usefulness of innovation as a holistic solution. Developing innovative solutions is not always related to technical bottlenecks, but is often caused by complex interplay and motivation.[66] The connection of internal innovation with external resources requires a process of corporate development. The value of innovation also comes into question, with the pursuit of innovation often diluting corporate value, and that innovation as a whole being a target, not a process.[67]

While the study of supply chain management often revolves around the concept of innovation, focusing strictly on the concept of innovation may not always be effective in evaluating competitiveness.

The Resource-Based View

By definition, the resource-vased view as a basis for the competitive advantage of a firm lies primarily in the application of a bundle of valuable tangible or intangible resources at the firm's disposal.[68, 69, 70, 71]

The principal development on the theory took place between the mid-1980s and mid-1990s, with the resource-based view emerging as one of the more influential and frequently cited theories in management analysis and framework theory. Contributions to the theory were made by many scholars in explaining, expanding, and defining a wide variety of relationships and practices within the scope of theory.

The fundamental goal of the framework is the pursuit of explaining and assessing the internal sources of a firm's sustained competitive advantage (SCA)—a central proposition, which suggests that if a firm is to achieve a state of SCA, it must acquire and control valuable, rare, non-substitutable resources and capabilities, while having surrounding elements in place to absorb and apply them.[72, 73]

The resource-based view has been used in a number of capacities, predominantly for investigating market dynamics and competitive advantages of firms within various areas.[74] From a larger perspective, corporate alliances present organizations with an opportunity to explore new competencies, thereby enabling supply chain integration and possibly automation, ultimately leading to a potential competitive advantage.

Within this theory, supply chain advantages can be measured and compared in terms of value presented within the entire chain. In relation to the study of supply chain management specifically, the resource-based theory emphasizes transaction cost efficiency as the motivating factor for strategic alliances among firms, and can therefore be used to demonstrate various areas of automation within supply chain management.

In considering supply chains as unit of analysis, supply chain processes are the same as routines,[75] in which these functions constitute the core purpose of supply chains. This approach considers the organization as a combination of strategy, structure, and process—each responsible for internal aspects of organization.

Within this perspective, supply chain resources and capabilities must be present within supply chain business processes, if not forming the core of the process. Further expansion has defined a business process as a set of structured activities with specified goals oriented to serve customers.[76] One often-accepted principle is that business processes are considered a method of integrating commerce functions.

Within these perspectives, the notion of competitiveness aligning through supply chain management can be observed. As we have noted the value of the supply chain as a competitive tool, the resource-based view presents itself as a meaningful method of examination. This assumption leads to a theory of business strategic goals impacting the overall success levels of a firm. To further this concept, often in assessing the strategic goals of supply chains, a great emphasis has been placed on environmental factors and less attention has been paid to unique characteristics of firms which are members of the chain and also the supply chains itself.[77] The ability of the resource-based view to account for environmental factors and competitive advantage is therefore well-founded.

By nature, the resource-based view is designed to complement and assess the competitiveness of an organization, with a number of prominent proponents noting its value.[78, 79] The pattern of the RBV in function is often to explicitly examine the internal sources of competitive advantage, and is by design aimed to explain why firms in the same industry might differ in performance.[80]

As noted, there may be a number of advantages and disadvantages to examining the competitiveness of a supply chain through the resource-based view.

The Knowledge-Based View

Although in many ways the resource-based view recognizes the important role of knowledge within a firm which achieves a competitive advantage, proponents of the knowledge-based view argue that the resource-based perspective does not go far enough.[81] Specifically, the resource-based view assumes knowledge to be a general and generic resource, as opposed to holding intrinsic and specific values,[82] and as such there is no clear identification of value through knowledge characteristics. The fundamental platform of the resource based theory is to assume that knowledge is a generic resource and not to recognize special characteristics or to distinguish between different types of knowledge-based capabilities.[83]

In many ways, the knowledge-based view is an extension of the resource-based view as it considers organizations as heterogeneous entities loaded with knowledge.[84] In contrast to the resource-based view, the knowledge-based theory of the firm considers knowledge as the most strategically significant resource of a firm. More attention is dedicated to the identification of differences and characteristics which may exist among various types of knowledge.[85] By design, the knowledge-based theory of the firm acknowledges knowledge as being the most strategically significant resource of a firm.[86] Other areas, including Information technologies, may also play an important role in the knowledge-based view of the firm, in that information systems can be used to synthesize, enhance, and expedite large-scale intra- and inter-firm knowledge management.[87] Within the realm of supply chain management competitiveness, this characteristic is noteworthy.

The theory as a fundamental process assumes that an organization's success is based on its ability to share the inherent knowledge embodied in organizational routines, and to transfer knowledge from one organizational unit to the other. This assumption is compounded by a growing pattern of supply chain organizations having the ability to share knowledge effectively from one unit to the other, with increased chances of survival as compared to organizations that are less adept at knowledge sharing.[88] The basis of the theory is to categorize knowledge sharing in two spheres based on the tacit-explicit dichotomy: soft and hard mechanisms.

Soft mechanisms entail transfer of tacit knowledge through face-to-face interface. In this view, knowledge sharing may be prioritized through the transfer of tacit knowledge. The exploration of this approach suggests that various methods are suitable for the transfer of tacit knowledge including apprenticeships, brainstorming camps, the use of metaphors and analogies, social networking, and learning by doing. Comparatively, it can also be argued that active direct communication between individuals acts as a means of sharing tacit knowledge. The core platform facilitates basic knowledge transfer through providing an environment for an organization's members to communicate.

The hard mechanism represents the transfer of explicit knowledge using information and communication technology. Proponents of hard mechanisms argue that information and communication technology enables the transmission of explicit knowledge to flow more seamlessly and allows for a vast array of knowledge transfer, thereby reducing time and space barriers.[89] Generally, there is need to tailor the type of knowledge being transferred so as to enhance efficiency and effectiveness across the transmission mechanism.

The success of corporations and organizations is greatly dependent on the interactions between flows of information, materials, manpower, and capital equipment.[90] Within the arena of supply chain management, the pattern of knowledge sharing is important as competitive advantages are often gained through collaboration.[91]

Areas of Vulnerability as a Result of Competitiveness

In the pursuit of being competitive, there are a number of areas for potential vulnerability within the supply chain. Examples of areas of vulnerability may include the following:

1. **Insufficient product design and/or poor quality-control standards**

   In an effort to reduce production and manufacturing costs, companies may engage in numerous strategies. Outsourcing and offshoring production is a viable method in which product manufacturing companies may take advantage of lower labor cost and less restrictive labor practices. While these practices may result in a lowered landed overall cost (even in consideration of transportation and tariffs etc.), the trade-off is a lack of production control, which can potentially result in a number of detrimental consequences, including loss of brand image, damaged relationships between vendors, and consumer injury.

   One popular example is the case of Mattel, who outsourced production of certain products to China. Concerns about lead-based paint and magnets which could become loose led to safety concerns and resulted in recalls of more than twenty million toys. The impact this recall had on Mattel's brand image, relationships with vendors, and ability to project demand in future periods was notable. The internal changes at Mattel which followed were also expensive and potentially detrimental to the business model—increased internal manufacturing, use of certified vendors, increased inspections etc.

Companies may also be inclined to expedite the speed of production and product design by not including certain product safety features in the product development and manufacturing stages. While these decisions may coincide with design standards and may be necessary for the business model overall, the risk to consumer safety is present.

2. **Incorrect and unsafe methods of storage of products**

One of the main functions and areas of consideration within a supply chain is the forecasting of demand. As such, finished and unfinished products are often held at various points of a chain (e.g., warehouses, distribution centers, retailer storage facilities, etc.) for strategic business purposes (e.g., hard product conversions, scheduled product launches, etc.), in an effort to meet perceived customer demand and to hedge against unanticipated demand fluctuation.

The storage of products could present the potential for vulnerability in terms of product quality. Certain products have specific storage requirements (e.g., temperature control during storage, stackability restrictions etc.). Further, different products have different degrees of obsolescence (e.g., laptop computers will devalue faster than T-shirts), and therefore the need to expedite the distribution and sale of product might contribute to poor storage standards and therefore product safety issues.

3. **Incorrect distribution and transportation of products**

As supply chains become more and more extensive, the need for transportation of product becomes more complex. Often supply chains rely on multiple methods of transport (e.g., freight, rail, truck, etc.). The use of multiple transportation methods may open the door for areas of vulnerability in terms of product quality and product safety.

One interesting example is liquid laundry detergent. If transported in non-heated trailers, there is a tendency for the liquid to freeze. When thawed, it often does not return to its original consistency. While this may not be a product safety concern (the product still functions as required), the image of the brand and the perceived level of product quality may suffer.

Over the past two decades, the practice of online purchasing has grown considerably. As such, the concepts of last-mile delivery and last-mile fulfilment (the final steps of delivery where product is delivered to a consumer's doorstep) have come into view. While this process seems relatively seamless, it involves a modification of the traditional retail-facing supply chain model, and could potentially allow product quality vulnerability as non-specialized delivery processes might be used.

4. **Incorrect packaging of products**

In many cases, the packaging of consumer products is designed to showcase the product function, present brand and marketing messages, and function as an efficient method to protect, store, and distribute the product. A number of considerations exist within the realm of product packaging, including the cost of packaging materials, stackability of products, size of packaged product, and environmental impact of packaging.

Many companies have adjusted packaging (and in many cases product size and specifications) as part of a larger business strategy. The goal of cost reduction through cheaper packaging is an easy to understand cost-saving strategy, which could contribute to potential product damage and therefore consumer injury.

One of the more controversial supply chain topics is the concept of "shrink." Shrink is the term used to explain missing product from a supply chain (e.g., a store buys ten units, but only sells eight units. Two units are missing). Traditionally it was assumed that the main contributing factor for shrink was customer theft (i.e., the missing two units were stolen). As such, in addition to other methods, many companies went through the process of increasing the size of packaging to discourage shoplifting. This in turn resulted in products being packaged to limit potential theft, which may not necessarily prioritize product safety and quality.

The practice of gaining a competitive advantage through supply chain management is not a new process; however, the areas of vulnerability to product safety, product quality, product longevity, and product sustainability are evident. The impact supply chain decisions (and therein business strategy decisions) have on product design, manufacturing, distribution, storage, and retail practices are visible within various industries, and are an important area of consideration in assessing consumer safeguards and overall wellbeing in the marketplace.

Notes

1. Innes, D. and LaLonde, B. (1994). "Customer service: The key to customer satisfaction, customer loyalty and market share." *Journal of Business Logistics* 15(1): 1–28.

2. Ibid.

3. Morehouse, J. and Bowersox, D. (1995). *Supply Chain Management: Logistics for the Future*. U.S. Food Marketing Institute.

4. Gunasekaran, A. and Ngai, E. W. T. (2005). "Build-to-order supply chain management: Literature review and framework for development." *Journal of Operations Management* 23(5): 423–451.

5. Cox, A. (2001). "The power perspective in procurement and supply chain management." *Journal of Supply Chain Management* 37(1): 4–7.

6. Chopra, S. and Meindl, P. (2002). *Supply Chain Management: Strategy, Planning, and Operations*. Prentice Hall.

7. Mentzer, J., DeWitt, W., Keebler, J., Min, S., Nix, N., Smith, C. and Zacharia, Z. (2001). "Defining Supply Chain Management." *Journal of Business Logistics* 22(2): 1–25.

8. Handfield, R. and Nichols, E. (1999). *Introduction to Supply Chain Management*. Prentice Hall.

9. Christopher, M. (1998). *Logistics and Supply Chain Management: Strategies for Reducing Costs and Improving Services*. Pitman Publishing.

10. Cox, A. (2001).

11. Cavinato, J. L. (1992). "A total cost/value model for supply chain competitiveness." *Journal of Business Logistics* 13(2): 285–301.

12. Cooper M. C. and Ellram L. M. (1993). "Characteristics of supply chain management and the implications for purchasing and logistics strategy." *International Journal of Logistics Management* 4(2): 13–24.

13. Gunasekaran, A. and Ngai, E. W. T. (2005).

14. Towill, D. R., Naim, M. M. and Wikner, J. (1992). "Industrial dynamics simulation models in the design of supply chains." *International Journal of Physical Distribution & Logistics Management* 22(5): 3–13.

15. Lee, H. L. (1996). "Effective inventory and service management through product and process redesign." *Operations Research* 44(1): 151–159.

16. Morehouse, J. and Bowersox, D. (1995). *Supply Chain Management: Logistics for the Future.* U.S. Food Marketing Institute.

17. Sako, M. (1993). *Prices, Quality and Trust: Inter-firm Relations in Britain and Japan.* Cambridge University Press.

18. Lee, H. and Billington, C. (1992). "Supply chain management: Pitfalls and opportunities." *Sloan Management Review* 33(3): 65–71.

19. Berry, D., Towill, D. R. and Wadsley, N. (1994). "Supply chain management in the electronics products industry." *International Journal of Physical Distribution and Logistics Management* 24(10): 20–32.

20. Cox, A. (2001).

21. Martin, C. (2005). *Logistics and Supply Chain Management: Strategies for Reducing Cost and Improving Service.* Financial Times Press.

22. Sako, M. (1993).

23. Balakrishnan, J. and Cheng, C. H. (2005). "The theory of constraints and the make-or-buy decision: An update and review." *The Journal of Supply Chain Management* 41(1): 40–47.

24. Daya, M., Hariga, M. and Khursheed, S.N. (2008). "Economic production quantity model with a shifting production rate." *International Transactions in Operational Research* 15(1): 87–101.

25. Salvetat, D. and Géraudel, M. (2012). "The tertius roles in a coopetitive context: The case of the European aeronautical and aerospace engineering sector." *European Management Journal* 30(6): 603–614.

26. Arlbjorn, J. S. (2011). "Logistics and supply chain management in a globalized economy." *International Journal of Physical Distribution & Logistics Management* 41(4): 340–342.

27. Baumgartner, H. and Pieter, R. (2003). "The structural influence of marketing journals: A citation analysis of the discipline and its subareas over time." *Journal of Marketing* 67(2): 123–139.

28. Gunasekaran, A. and Ngai, E. W. T. (2005).

29. Burgess K., Singh, O. J. and Koroglu, R. (2006). "Supply chain management: A structured literature review and implications for future research." *International Journal of Operations and Production Management* 26(7): 703–729.

30. Carter, C. R. and Ellram, L. M. (2003). "Thirty-five years of The Journal of Supply Chain Management: Where have we been and where are we going?" *The Journal of Supply Chain Management* (39)2: 27–40.

31. Bommer, M., O'Neil, B. and Treat, S. (2001). "Strategic assessment of the supply chain interface: a beverage industry case study." *International Journal of Physical Distribution and Logistics Management* 31(1): 11–25.

32. Thatte, A. A., Rao, S. and Ragu-Nathan T. S. (2013). "Impact of SCM practices of a firm on supply chain responsiveness and competitive advantage of a firm." *The Journal of Applied Business Research* 29(2): 499–530.

33. Salvetat, D. and Géraudel, M. (2012).

34. Holl, A. (2004). "Start-Ups and Relocations: Manufacturing plant location in Portugal." *Regional Science Association International* 83(4): 649–668.

35. Chang, P. and Lin, H. (2015). "Manufacturing plant location selection in logistics network using analytic hierarchy process." *Journal of Industrial Engineering and Management* 8(5): 1547–1575.

36. Doeringer, P., Evans-Klock, C. and Terkla, D. (2005). "Management cultures and regional development: High performance management and the location of new manufacturing plants." *European Planning Studies* 13(6): 815–830.

37. Lu, D. (2011). *Fundamentals of Supply Chain Management*. Ventus Publishing APS.

38. Daskin, M. S., Snyder, L. V. and Berger, R. T. (2003). "Facility location in supply chain design." Working Paper No. 03-010. Northwestern University.

39. Bartlett, M. S. (1954). "A note on multiplying factors for various chi-squared approximations." *Journal of the Royal Statistical Society* 16(2): 296–298.

40. Penrose, E. T. (1959). *The Theory of the Growth of the Firm.* Wiley Publishing.

41. Guttman, L. A. (1954). *A New Approach to Factor Analysis: Mathematical Thinking in Social Sciences.* Columbia University Press.

42. Kaiser, H. F. (1974). "An index of factorial simplicity." *Psychometrika* 39(1): 31–36.

43. McFadden, D. (1974). "Conditional logit analysis of qualitative choice behavior." In P. Zarembka (ed.), *Frontiers in Econometrics.* Academic Press. 105–142.

44. Gunasekaran, A., Patel, C. and McGaughey, R. E. (2004). "A framework for supply chain performance measurement." *International Journal of Production Economics* 87(3): 333–347.

45. Bourlakis, M. A. and Weightman, P. W. (2008). *Food Supply Chain Management.* Blackwell Publishing.

46. Collier, D. A. and Evans, J. R. (2011). *Operations Management.* Cengage Learning.

47. Langley, C. J., Gibson, B. J., Novack, R. A. and Bardi, E. J. (2008). *Supply Chain Management: A Logistics Perspective.* Cengage Learning.

48. Lee, W. B. and Katzorke, M. (2010). *Leading Effective Supply Chain Transformations: A Guide to Sustainable World-class Capability and Results.* J. Ross Publishing.

49. Wisner, J. D., Tan, K. and Leong, G. K. (2008). *Principles of Supply Chain Management with Infotrac: A Balanced Approach.* Cengage Learning.

50. Collier, D. A. and Evans, J. R. (2011).

51. Lu, D. (2011).

52. Collier, D. A. and Evans, J. R. (2011).

53. Current, J., Ratick, S. and ReVelle, C. (1998). "Dynamic facility location when the total number of facilities in uncertain: A decision analysis approach." *European Journal of Operational Research* 110(3): 597–609.

54. Erlebacher, S. J. and Meller, R. D. (2000). "The interaction of location and inventory in designing distribution systems." *IIE Transactions* 32(2): 155–166.

55. Daskin, M. S., Snyder, L. V. and Berger, R. T. (2003).

56. Jornsten, K. and Bjorndal, M. (1994). "Dynamic location under uncertainty." *Studies in Regional and Urban Planning* 1(3): 163–184.

57. Geoffrion, A. M. and Powers, R. F. (1980). "Facility location analysis is just the beginning (if you do it right)." *Interfaces* 1(2): 22–30.

58. Morehouse, J. and Bowersox, D. (1995).

59. Anderson, D. L., Britt, F. E. and Favre, D. J. (1997). "The seven principles of supply chain management." *Supply Chain Management Review* (Summer): 19–26.

60. Guinipero, L., Hooker, R., Joseph-Matthews, S., Yoon, T. and Brudvig, S. (2008). "A decade of SCM literature: Past, present and future implications." *Journal of Supply Chain Management* 44(4): 66–86.

61. Dyer J. (1996). "Specialized supplier networks as a source of competitive advantage." *Strategic Management Journal* 17(4): 271–291.

62. Gulati, R., Nohria, N. and Zaheer, A., (2000). "Special issue: Strategic networks." *Strategic Management Journal* 21(3): 191–201.

63. Jarillo, J. C. (1988). "On strategic networks." *Strategic Management Journal* 9(1): 31–41.

64. Heinrichs, J. H. and Lim, J. S. (2003). "Integrating web-based data mining tools with business models for knowledge management." *Decision Support Systems* 35(1): 103–112.

65. Leonard, D., and Sensiper, S. (1998). "The role of tacit knowledge in group innovation." *California Management Review* 40(3): 112–132.

66. Katz, C. (2004). *Growing Up Global: Economic Restructuring and Children's Everyday Lives*. University of Minnesota Press.

67. Vanhaverbeke, W. and Cloodt, M. (2006). "Open innovation in value networks." In H. Chesbrough, and W. P. M. Vanhaverbeke (Eds.), *Open Innovation: Researching a New Paradigm*. Oxford University Press. 258–281.

68. Penrose, E. T. (1959).

69. Rumelt, R. (1984). "Towards a strategic theory of the firm." In: R. Lamb, Ed., *Competitive Strategic Management*. Prentice-Hall. 556–570.

70. Wernerfelt, B. (1984). "A resource-based view of the firm." *Strategic Management Journal* 5(2): 171–180.

71. Mwailu, M. I. and Mercer, K. (1983). "Human resource scorecard: A road map to balanced scorecard." *World Journal of Social Sciences* 4(1): 70–79.

72. Barney, J. (1991). "Firm resources and sustained competitive advantages." *Journal of Management* 17(1): 99–120.

73. Barney, J. (2001). "Is the resource-based "view" a useful perspective for strategic management research? Yes." *Academy of Management Review* 26(1): 41–56.

74. Mwailu, M. I. and Mercer, K. (1983).

75. Nelson, R. and Winter, S. (1982). *An Evolutionary Theory of Economic Change*. Harvard University Press.

76. Davenport, T. H. and Prusak, L. (1998). *Working Knowledge: How Organizations Manage What They Know*. Harvard Business School Press.

77. Miles, R. and Snow, C. (1978). *Organizational Strategy, Structure, and Process*. McGraw-Hill Publishing.

78. Bain, J. S. (1968). *Industrial Organization*. John Wiley Publishing.

79. Porter, M. (1985). *Competitive Advantage*. The Free Press.

80. Handfield, R. and Nichols, E. (1999).

81. Grant, R. M. (1996). "Toward a knowledge-based theory of the firm." *Strategic Management Journal* 17: 109–122.

82. Alavi, M. and Leidner, D. E. (2001). "Knowledge management systems: Emerging views and practices from the field." Conference Publication: 32nd Hawaii International Conference on System Sciences, Maui, HI, USA, 5–8 Jan. 1999, IEEE.

83. Foss, N. (1996). "More critical comments on knowledge-based theories of the firm." *Organization Science* 7(5): 519 523.

84. Hoskisson, R. E., Hitt, M. A., Wan, W. P. and Yiu, D. (1999). "Theory and research in strategic management: Swings of a pendulum." *Journal of Management* 25(3): 417–456.

85. Grant, R. M. (1996).

86. Conner, K. R. (1991). "A historical comparison of resource-based theory and five schools of thought within industrial organization economics: Do we have a new theory of the firm?" *Journal of Management* 17(1): 121–153.

87. Alavi, M. and Leidner, D. E. (2001).

88. Spender, J. C. (1996). "Making knowledge the basis of a dynamic theory of the firm." *Strategic Management Journal* 17: 45–62.

89. Nonaka, I. and Takeuchi, H. (1995). *The Knowledge Creating Company: How Japanese Companies Create the Dynamics of Innovation*. Oxford University Press.

90. Salvetat, D. and Géraudel, M. (2012).

91. Arlbjorn, J. S. (2011). "Logistics and supply chain management in a globalized economy." *International Journal of Physical Distribution & Logistics Management* 41(4): 340–342.